The Mysterious Mansion

Contributing Authors

Queen of Heaven Catholic Elementary School- Milton, ON

Mrs. Rose Grundy's Grade 3 Class:

Henry Aas

Clara Afonso

Ella Brennan

Tristan Bucknor

Gabriella Chagas

Quinn Charles-Wiltshire

Alex D.

Sawyer Fortier

Valentina Martinez

Alessandra Middleton

Makayla Miguel

Colbie Murray

David Emmanuel Ocol

Alexandra Rich

Matthew Rico

Tyler Soares

Kaiya Torreno

Sofia Vieira

Michaela Zareski

Contributing Authors

Queen of Heaven Catholic Elementary School- Milton, ON

Miss. Christine Dief's Grade 3 Class:

London Atendido	Tegan Leong
Nezzelle Blair	Leah Loconte
Malcolm Brown	Massimo Lomangino
Cayla Cardoso	Aidan Martin
Jordan Duguay	Jaiden Melino
Ross Fraser	Deilani Riquelme
Sofia Fuda	Alyssa Ross
Sebastian Glaz	Bella Rusak
Zaiden Hraiche	Jacob Urbaniak

Contributing Authors

Queen of Heaven Catholic Elementary School- Milton, ON

Miss. Lauren Pellicciotta's Grade 3 Class:

Vivian Bressette	Krista McEwan
Josh Carter	Joseph Mendes
Sophia Chin	Addison Moodie
Leeton Dabu	Mateo Ordonez
Jana Dowds	Gavin Putzu
Ethan A.	Isabella Rodrigues
Fernandes	Meagan Trinh
Skyler Hourani	Xander Wright
Ryan da Costa	Sasha Zajac
	Gabriella Chiarotto

Contributing Authors

Queen of Heaven Catholic Elementary School- Milton, ON

Mrs. Michelle Digout's Grade 3 Class:

Natalia Arias Alfaro	Paulina Padtykalava
Gabriel Camaya	Sloan Roettger
Hailey Corpuz	Ethan Smith
Orion de Vera	Makayla Supple
Tess Dos Anjos	Tomasz Swietoniewski
Hailey Fernandes	Kate Theodoulou
Joshua Fernandes	Owen Radman-O'Connor
Kiara Giannuzzi	Psalm Tongol
Aidan MacLellan	Logan Victoria

Contributing Authors

Queen of Heaven Catholic Elementary School- Milton, ON

Ms. Kaylyn Dorland's Grade 3 Class:

Ciara Buchanan

Olivia Burton

Sebastien Cesaer

Peter Celec

Darien Delevante

Joshua Ditommaso

Rianne Drew

Adrienne Fernandez

Austin Jones

Isabelle Juan

Ferdie Magallanes

Temi Mayuku

Samuel Ramos

Miah Rumble

Serena Silva

Marin Toneatti

Katerina Vander Holt

Jaymeson Warner

ACKNOWLEGMENTS

A very special thank you to all those who help make Write to Give happen. Each year, the program continues to grow and have a bigger impact on Canadian and international students. This would not happen, if it were not for the hard work of the teachers who have helped implement this program.

Thank you to our teachers, Rose Grundy, Christine Dief, Lauren Pellicciotta, Michelle Digout and Kaylyn Dorland.

Thank you to my team of editors, designers and family who have helped with W2G 2018.

Thank you,

Amy McLaren

viii

The Mysterious Mansion

It was a damp and rainy day and the sky was filled with fog. Five curious Grade 3 friends were walking home from school on a gloomy Thursday.

Suddenly, the fog cleared, and they could see in the distance a creepy and run down looking mansion.

"Where in the world did that come from?" Walter said.

"Maybe we should go check it out and see if anyone lives there!" Angelina said excitedly.

"I don't think that's a good idea because our parents will be worried if we're not home soon," said Luca.

"Are you chicken, Luca?" Angelina teased.

"It could be the start of a new adventure!" Alyson added.

"I've never seen this house before. It could be fun to check it out." Marco agreed. "Oh, alright fine, but I'm not staying for long!" Luca added.

When they walked through the squeaky door, it slammed behind them!

"Uggghh guys, the door is locked!!" Luca said with a shiver.

"Stop being a baby, Luca. The door is not locked!" said Angelina as she reached for the doorknob.

"Uh oh, guys, Luca was right. The door really is locked!!!" she said nervously.

Walter reached for the doorknob in a panic and frantically tried to open it.

CLUNK! Suddenly the doorknob fell off and hit the ground.

All five students stood silently and stared at the doorknob lying on the floor.

Luca began to argue, "I knew we never should have come in here!!! This is ALL your fault, Angelina!"

Marco agreed, "How are we going to get out of here now?"

"Don't blame this on Angelina! She didn't force us to come in here. Walter is the one who broke the doorknob!" added Alyson.

"Guys stop arguing! We need to find a way out of this creepy mansion." said Angelina.

"Yeah," added Walter "we need to work together to get out of this disaster!"

They began to look around the old dusty hallway to find a way out. The room was filled with paintings on every wall. As Angelina was looking under one of the frames, she noticed a note with a riddle on it. It said,

"Use the paintings in this room
They will guide you to a clue.
Be quick, be smart and always be clever,
This room will help you, if you work together!"

"It's an escape room!" Marco shouted. "What does that mean?" Luca said with a worry.

"It means that we need to solve all the riddles on the paintings, so we can break out of here!" exclaimed Angelina.

"Where's the first clue?" Walter asked. "This painting has the number one on it and it's a portrait of a scientist." Alyson replied.

All of a sudden, the painting of the scientist started to talk, "Hello, boys and girls, I have a question for you, what invention allows you to see through any wall?"

"X-ray goggles!" Walter answered.

"Those only exist in science-fiction books, Walter, but good try!

Ok, I know, a window!" Angelina shouted. "That's it!" They all agreed and ran towards the only window in the house, only to find out that it was sealed shut.

Just then Luca peered out the window, "Hey guys! Look over there!" Luca exclaimed.

All five children glanced out the foggy window to see an overgrown garden, with the words scribed in the dirt:

"Buried beneath the ground, is the painting to be found."

"What does that even mean?" Alyson asked hesitantly.

"Oh, I know," Marco responded excitedly. "Since we can't get outside to dig in the dirt the next clue must be in the basement!"

At that moment they all turned to see a steep, decrepit, wooden staircase leading to a dark, dusty basement. Clutching each other's hands, they tiptoed down the creaky steps and made their way into the darkness.

As they walked, a series of glowing footprints appeared and illuminated a path for them to follow. It came to an abrupt stop in front of an old, stone fireplace. Sitting on top of the mantle was a tattered painting, which read:

"*Sharing ideas and listening too; working together to see it through. When working together, you get things done, working together is so much fun! The clue to going home is hidden behind the stone.*"

Walter, Marco, Alyson, Luca and Angelina turned to each other with confused looks on their faces.

"I have an idea!" shouted Marco. "Maybe if we all work together and push on the different stones we can finally get out of here."

"It's worth a try, Marco," Angelina responded excitedly.

Just then all five children started using their hands to push on the cold, damp rocks which made up the fireplace.

Minutes passed, and then a loud boom echoed through the room.

The stone Alyson had been pushing on caused the fireplace to turn, unveiling a long narrow tunnel with a dim light at the end of it.

All together, they burst out into a loud cheer! "We did it!" Alison shouted cheerfully.

"This must be it, we just have to follow the light!" Walter said enthusiastically. "It's a good thing we'll be home just in time for dinner!

Man, I'm so hungry!" Marco replied.

"ME TOO!" The other four cried simultaneously.

They made their way out of the tunnel, past their school, and into the neighbourhood they all lived in. It was almost as though the mysterious mansion was just a dream.

"We really do make a great team! We couldn't have done this without working together." Walter announced.

"You know something, you're right! We can solve anything, when we work together," said Luca.

"Well that certainly was an adventure!" Alyson said.

"It always is with us," Marco responded. "It always is!"

WORLD TEACHER AID

World Teacher Aid is a Canadian charity committed to improving education throughout the developing world with a focus on IDP settlements (Internally Displaced Persons – communities that have been uprooted from their homes). Our current projects are within Kenya and Ghana.

As a charity we are committed to providing access to education for students within settled IDP Camps. We accomplish this vision through the renovation and/or construction of schools.

Before we begin working with a community, we ensure that they are on board with the goal. A community must be settled and show leadership before we commit to a project. We also look for commitment from the Government, ensuring that if we step in and build the school, that they will help support the ongoing expenses, such as teachers salaries, and more.

AUTOGRAPHS

Tess

Natalia

22

AUTOGRAPHS

AUTOGRAPHS

Made in the USA
Columbia, SC
04 June 2018